SHIRE NATURAL H

CU0096·1007

THE BLACKCAP
AND THE
GARDEN WARBLER

ERNEST GARCIA

CONTENTS

Cover: *A male blackcap broods tiny young. Stinging nettles provide added protection for this nest.*

Series editor: Jim Flegg.

Printed in Great Britain by C. I. Thomas & Sons (Haverfordwest) Ltd, Press Buildings, Merlins Bridge, Haverfordwest, Dyfed.

Warblers

The true warblers (Sylviidae) are a highly diverse family of insectivorous songbirds widespread in the woodland, scrubland and grassland habitats of the Old World. Some occur also in the Americas and Australasia but other warbler families dominate those continents. The family is a large and varied one of some 350 species and it is not easy to find a typical representative. However, most warblers are small or tiny birds, with fine, pointed bills. Some tropical species, such as many of the tailorbirds of Asia and the African apalises, are colourful but most warblers are soberly plumaged in green, brown, grey or yellow. In temperate regions especially warblers are far more conspicuous on account of their songs than their appearance. The family includes many distinguished songsters although only a minority actually warble, that is, produce a continuous gentle trilling sound. The Sylviidae are closely related to three other families, the thrushes (Turdidae), flycatchers (Muscicapidae) and the babblers (Timaliidae). They differ from the first two in having an unspotted juvenile plumage and they are smaller and less sociable than most babblers, but firmer distinctions between these families are impossible.

The genus *Sylvia*, with eighteen species, is largely confined to Europe, the Middle East and Western Asia in the breeding season. *Sylvia* species are commonly called scrub warblers and as such they are particularly typical of the evergreen maquis of the Mediterranean countries. Here, and within the woodlands inhabited elsewhere by other Sylvia species, they form part of a broader community of similar birds. For example, during the breeding season an area of mixed woodland in Britain may be expected to support goldcrests (*Regulus regulus*), chiffchaffs (*Phylloscopus collybita*), willow warblers (*P. trochilus*), wood warblers (*P. sibilatrix*), grasshopper warblers (*Locustella naevia*), blackcaps (*Sylvia atricapilla*), garden warblers (*S. borin*), whitethroats (*S. communis*) and lesser whitethroats (*S. curruca*), as well as a range of other insectivorous species including thrushes, flycatchers and tits.

Several studies have looked into how such 'guilds' of species divide up habitats between themselves and how different warblers manage to coexist, since they are all competing for the same fundamental resource: insects. Often, subtle differences between species in habitat preferences and in feeding techniques allow them to live together peacefully. However, those warblers which migrate south to avoid northern winters seem to be adaptable to a range of habitats and food sources. They need to be, since they meet a diversity of habitats when on passage and they usually winter in very different environments to those in which they breed. Still, it is typical of warblers that different species confine themselves to particular habitats, both when breeding and wintering, and exploit them in particular ways. It is becoming clear that this dividing up of resources is often due to competition between the different species, with some keeping out others from places in which they would otherwise be perfectly able to survive.

Competition for space is well known in *Sylvia* warblers and tends to be most severe where the species involved are most similar. Blackcaps and garden warblers have been found to interact strongly where they meet, so much so that an account of the ecology of one species really needs to take considerable notice of that of the other. For this reason, this book considers the two species together.

Blackcaps and garden warblers

STRUCTURE

Blackcaps (*Sylvia atricapilla*) and garden warblers (*Sylvia borin*) are among the larger *Sylvia* warblers but they are virtually identical in weight and some dimensions. During the breeding season both weigh about 17 grams but they become much heavier, exceptionally over 30 grams, when they lay down fat reserves before migration. Garden warblers have the long pointed wings typical of long-distance migrants. Their wing lengths, of about 77 mm on average, are some 3 mm longer than those of blackcaps, many of which migrate over comparatively short distances. The resident blackcaps of the Mediterranean region, and also those other non-migratory populations on the Canary Islands and other Atlantic archipelagoes, have even shorter, more rounded wings than their migratory northern counterparts. Blackcaps have slightly longer tails than garden warblers, a difference which is sometimes obvious to the experienced eye seeing birds in flight, when blackcap tails also look narrower.

The species differ in their moult strategies. Typically, garden warblers moult completely in winter quarters although some birds, especially from Britain, have been known to complete a wing moult before departure. Blackcaps moult chiefly on the breeding grounds, between July and September, before migrating south.

Garden warbler bills are slightly shorter, broader and deeper than those of blackcaps, and they look stouter in the field. The stubby-billed appearance of garden warblers is a good fieldmark and sets them apart from other nondescript medium-sized warblers, such as marsh warblers (*Acrocephalus palustris*), with which they are sometimes confused. Among warblers generally, differences in bill structure are associated with significant differences in diet, but these have yet to be demonstrated between these two species. Blackcaps have slightly longer tarsi than garden warblers, but both are the shortest-legged of all *Sylvia* warblers. Short legs are associated with an arboreal way of life and the fact that the two species are similar in this respect emphasises that they are adapted to similar habitats.

PLUMAGE

Blackcaps are distinctive and the two sexes are easily separated by plumage. Males have black crowns but those of females are a warm brown. Males are greyish-olive above and greyish-white below. Females are similar but browner above and more buffish below. The bills are slaty-black and the legs dark grey. The juveniles resemble females but they are browner above and yellowish below and their crowns are a muddier-brown colour. Juvenile males acquire their black caps over their first winter and some still show brown foreheads or scattered brown crown feathers during their first breeding season.

The outpost blackcap populations from Madeira and the Canary Islands, but not apparently those from the Azores or the Cape Verde Islands, tend to be darker than mainland birds, with a brown wash on the flanks of both sexes. A melanistic form, in which the males have a completely black head and throat and underparts which are a uniform olive-brown or even black, occurs in the Azores and Madeira and is also known, more rarely, from the Canary Islands.

By contrast, garden warblers are among the plainest of passerines, with no striking field marks. Unlike most *Sylvia* warblers, the sexes are identical in plumage. Both are a fairly uniform mousy grey-brown, shading to a warm buff beneath. In fresh plumage, an area of paler grey on the sides of the neck is worth looking for. There is also a hint of a pale stripe above the eye. Juveniles are slightly browner than adults, with a faint yellowish cast below. The bill is grey. The dark eye is shared with blackcaps but stands out in this species, probably because of the pale crown and face of garden warblers. The chunky, round-headed, stubby-billed appearance is also subtly distinctive, as are the pale blue-grey legs and feet. Nevertheless, garden warblers are often misidentified, especially when found in unexpected surroundings. Many a novice ringer has identified a garden warbler caught in a reed bed as a member of the genus *Acrocephalus*! Presumably garden warblers derive some advantage from a lack of sexual dimorphism but what this is has yet to be discovered.

HABITATS

The geographical ranges of the two species overlap extensively but not completely. In the breeding season garden warblers extend further north than blackcaps, into the subarctic birch zone. The ranges are quite different in the Mediterranean area, where the garden warbler is largely absent or restricted to mountain forests and the blackcap is widespread and locally common. Presumably straying migrants have given rise to the isolated, resident populations of blackcaps found on the Azores, Madeira, the Canary Islands and, within the tropics, on the Cape Verde Islands. Garden warblers are absent from all these Atlantic islands.

Where the ranges overlap the two species are often found in similar habitats. Both favour open deciduous woodland, especially where there is a dense understorey of bramble and other shrubs. Hawthorn and blackthorn scrub is also favoured by both species, but here garden warblers typically predominate. Hedgerows are also used by both species provided they include trees or tall shrubs. Some dense ground cover for nesting is required by both species and closed deciduous forests or conifer stands with little understorey tend to be avoided. However, young conifer plantations, which may have a dense scrubby undergrowth, and the open spruce forests of central Europe are attractive to both species. In Germany such evergreen vegetation has been found to be valuable to early-nesting blackcaps, which may start breeding before deciduous cover has fully developed in the spring, since nests in conifers are relatively sheltered from the weather and from predators. Garden warblers have no special association with gardens and only large ones with a woodland or scrub component are likely to attract either species.

All garden warblers, and most blackcaps, are migratory but the two species have largely separate winter quarters. Garden warblers are entirely trans-Saharan migrants. In winter they are found in a range of deciduous and evergreen forest communities in Africa and they are one of the few Eurasian migrants which regularly inhabit mountain rain forests there, mainly frequenting the forest edges. Some blackcaps occur together with garden warblers in humid evergreen forests but garden warblers extend much further south than most blackcaps and are common in South Africa. Blackcaps have substantial wintering populations much further north, in Eritrea and in the belt of acacia steppe across sub-Saharan west Africa. More strikingly, very large numbers of blackcaps, perhaps the majority of the European populations, winter in the Mediterranean area, except in the relatively arid south-eastern portion, north-European birds joining the mainly sedentary local ones.

Blackcaps are structurally adapted to wintering in colder climates than garden warblers, having a winter plumage which is denser and about 20 per cent heavier than that of the garden warbler. This has no doubt helped those blackcaps which increasingly have been wintering in Britain and northwest Europe, encouraged perhaps by a succession of mild winters and the ready availability of food on garden bird-tables. Blackcaps wintering in cold climates, as in Britain, make a physiological adjustment in maintaining significantly higher fat reserves than do those in the usual winter quarters. Blackcaps weighed in Britain in January averaged 21 grams, compared with 18 grams for those caught in the same month in southern Spain. The additional reserves are probably essential if the birds are to cope with the low temperatures of a British winter and especially with the short days, which limit the amount of time available for finding food.

FOOD AND FEEDING

Both species are predominantly insectivorous but fruits are important in their diet at certain seasons. They are both foliage gleaners, given to searching meticulously through trees and bushes for settled insects but rather seldom engaging in more vigorous hunting techniques, such as flycatching. This is probably because they are relatively large warblers and most of the prey which can be caught in flight is too small to warrant the effort which would be needed to capture it. In contrast, relatively tiny warblers, such as

1. *A male blackcap. This is a young bird since it still shows some juvenile brown crown feathers.*

2. *A female blackcap drinking. The rufous cap distinguishes it from a male.*

3. *A garden warbler at the nest, showing well the stubby beak and the faint eye stripe.*

chiffchaffs, find it economical to dart and hover after even tiny insects, such as midges.

Similar warbler species are often known to avoid competition by specialising in foraging for food at different levels in woodlands and forests. There is no evidence that this occurs between blackcaps and garden warblers. On the contrary, one study in an English wood found that during the breeding season the two species hunted in similar places in the undergrowth and trees. Both found food mainly at levels below 6 metres but neither species avoided the highest levels of the canopy and they both often foraged there, especially when caterpillars were abundant on oaks in May. An Italian study, which recorded the heights at which birds were captured in mist nets set in homogeneous scrub, found that the two species did not differ in this respect, again suggesting that the two forage at similar heights.

In Britain, the first blackcaps to arrive in late March and April do so at a time when the main tree species are still in bud and foliage is limited to the bramble ground layer, ivy and certain shrubs. Nevertheless, insects probably already form the main part of the diet at this time, although ivy berries are also eaten if available and certain individuals like to take nectar from the flowers of goat willow. The aphids which cover the sycamore buds in spring are also a favoured food early in the season. Garden warblers arrive in late April and May, when the foliage is better developed and insects are abundant.

Both species feed their young chiefly on caterpillars, which are extremely important in the diet of most woodland birds in May. Pairs raising second broods, and in Britain these are almost exclusively blackcaps, have to find alternative foods, and flies and beetles are then taken extensively. Both usually take substantial and relatively slow-moving flies, such as crane flies (Tipulidae) and march flies (Bibionidae), rather than smaller items such as midges and gnats. The beetles may even include ladybirds (Coccinellidae), which are sometimes eaten in numbers, despite their reputed distastefulness, but only when caterpillars are not available. A wide range of insect orders, and also spiders and other arachnids, figure in the diet of both species and other small animals such as woodlice are also taken. Both species occasionally eat tiny snails and they feed them regularly to their young, perhaps as a calcium supplement.

Fruits, notably those of elder, are eaten by both birds in quantity during and before the autumn migration. In northern Europe fruit is only a supplement to the diet since both species lose weight rapidly and die if fed exclusively on north European fruits. However, blackcaps wintering in the Mediterranean area are predominantly frugivorous as the olive, fig, lentisc, buckthorn and other fruits available there in winter are relatively nutritious, with a high fat and protein content. For example, pulp from the berries of 21 species of Spanish shrubs eaten by birds contained an average of 10.2 per cent dry weight of fat, compared with 3.3. to 4.6 per cent for the pulps of six fruits commonly taken in England.

The minority of blackcaps which winter in Britain and northwest Europe rely heavily on fruits, including those of cotoneaster, ivy, holly and mistletoe, and on exotic foods such as bread, fat and peanuts, which they find on garden bird-tables. These birds probably spend the late autumn in woodlands since they only become common in gardens from December onwards, as the weather becomes colder, and cold spells bring an increased number of records of birds at garden feeders. Remarkably, some of these blackcaps have learnt to cling tit-fashion to suspended baskets of peanuts, a feeding strategy very untypical of any warbler.

In taking to bird-table fare, blackcaps have shown an unsuspected versatility in diet and behaviour. Another example is often seen in Gibraltar, where the large numbers of wintering blackcaps turn to nectar-eating in winters when the olive crop is poor. The preferred source of this nectar is the introduced South African succulent *Aloe arborescens*, which is normally pollinated by sunbirds (Nectariniidae) in its native home. The aloes grow in clumps and some blackcaps regularly take up territory there, driving off all comers who may try to deplete the nectar supply. The blackcaps feed by clinging to the flower spikes and inserting their beaks into the corollas. Blackcap beaks are far shorter than those of sunbirds, which are purpose-built for nectarivory, but nevertheless they do succeed in reaching the nectar.

4. *The breeding and wintering ranges of blackcaps.*

5. *The breeding and wintering ranges of garden warblers.*

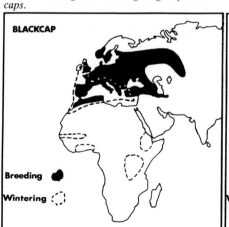

A garden warbler examined in Sweden in May had eaten 86 hawthorn stamens, and the faeces of a blackcap handled in Britain in late July contained over 300 unidentified anthers, showing that both species will take plant material other than berries and nectar, at least occasionally.

The diet of both species in African winter quarters has not been studied in detail but again, as well as insects, many fruits are taken, including those of figs, *Salvadora*, *Treema* and many others, some of them exotics such as mulberries and *Lantana*.

It would be interesting to know whether the diet of both species differs enough to reduce competition between them where they occur together. The available information, however, suggests that both are opportunists and will take a broad and similar range of food items according to availability. There is no evidence that either specialises closely on any one type of invertebrate or plant food, still less that the two species differ importantly in diet at the time when they are in contact with each other on the breeding grounds.

Breeding

BREEDING SEASONS

Considerable information is available on the breeding of both species in Britain from the long-standing Nest Record card scheme operated by the British Trust for Ornithology. Here, although many blackcaps establish territories during April, very few get down to nesting in that month and the peak blackcap laying period only begins 20 to 25 days after the first nests are started. Garden warblers arrive some three weeks later than blackcaps but they settle comparatively rapidly, the peak laying period being 10 to 15 days after the first nests are started. This means that the breeding seasons of the two overlap extensively and competition between them can be expected to be high at this time. Probably both species base their breeding cycle chiefly around the period of peak abundance of caterpillars on oaks and other deciduous trees. The seasonal glut of *Tortrix*, winter moth and

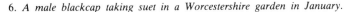

6. *A male blackcap taking suet in a Worcestershire garden in January.*

7. *A garden warbler in flight. The dark eye stands out against the sober, brownish plumage.*

other caterpillars must then make it relatively easy to feed the young. There may be a trend for the breeding seasons of the two to overlap even more closely. Nest Record cards show that in Britain during 1949 to 1963, 10.8 per cent of blackcap nests were started in April. However, during 1964 to 1978, this proportion declined to 1.4 per cent, perhaps as a result of a series of colder than average springs.

The tropical blackcaps of the Cape Verde Islands have adopted a breeding cycle which suits the local climate and which is quite unlike that of any other population. Birds begin laying before the first rains, at the end of July, but stop by the end of November, when cold trade winds interrupt breeding. They have a second extended breeding season from late January until June, when humid weather again makes a high number of insects available.

COURTSHIP AND NESTS

Both species build open, cup-shaped nests low down in dense vegetation. Most nests are between 0.5 m and 1.5 m from the ground, typically well hidden, especially in brambles and also in nettles, elder, hawthorn or blackthorn. The nests are of grass stems and thin twigs, with a lining of fine roots and hair. Those of blackcaps tend to be more compact than garden warbler nests and, on average, the latter are built lower down. However, the nests of the two species are not safely distinguishable.

Blackcap and garden warbler males build cock nests. Sometimes these are scrappy affairs involving a few pieces of grass but others may amount to half the size of a completed nest. Cock nest construction may begin before the females arrive and later may play a part in courtship. Courting males make themselves conspicuous to the females, chasing them and singing long bursts of song. They may attract the females by raising their crown feathers and gently fanning their wings and flirting their tails. Blackcaps seem particularly excitable when courting and are even known to hang upside down from twigs when showing off to a hoped-for mate.

Once a male has attracted the attention of a female he often tries to lead her to a cock nest, flying ahead of her and making himself conspicuous at the nest site, perhaps with a grass stem held demonstratively in his beak. Once a bird has been accepted by a mate, the female may cooperate with the male in building a finished nest. Many garden warbler females, and at least some female blackcaps, select and complete one of their mate's cock nests. Others build a completely new nest. In blackcaps, at least, most of the real work of nest-building is done by the female. If a second clutch is laid this is usually within a new nest.

EGGS AND YOUNG

Clutch sizes of both species are smaller in the south of their ranges than further north. Extensive information is available from Britain, where blackcaps typically have slightly larger clutches than garden warblers. A blackcap nest most often has five eggs but garden warblers have clutches of four eggs almost as often as those of five. Both species may lay as many as seven eggs, but this is exceptional. Clutches of fewer than four eggs are usually replacement or second clutches. As with the nests, the eggs of the two species are not always distinguishable with certainty. They both vary considerably, having a pale buff or greyish-white ground colour usually blotched and spotted with darker markings. Such markings are typically better defined on garden warbler eggs than on those of blackcaps. An erythristic form, where the ground colour is pink, is not infrequent in blackcaps and is also known in garden warbler clutches.

Once clutches have been completed both species enjoy a high hatching success, about 70 per cent in Britain. Survival to fledging is also very high, about 80 per cent in both species. Only a small proportion of blackcaps and garden warblers raise second broods. In Britain these are more frequent among black-

8. *The breeding seasons of blackcaps and garden warblers in Britain. The graphs show the dates of laying of the first eggs, grouped by five day periods.*

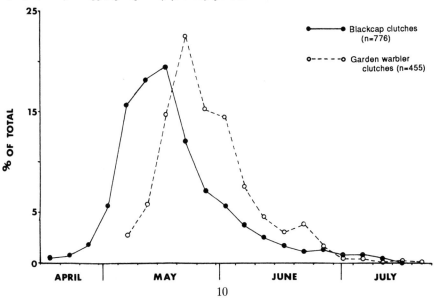

9. *A male blackcap feeds its brood.*

Songs and calls

SONGS

Blackcaps and garden warblers are reputed to have very similar songs which some people find difficult to tell apart. Certainly the songs are similar, at least sometimes, but they have distinctive features which usually help to separate them. Some *Sylvia* warblers have fairly stereotyped songs. For example, the lesser whitethroat (*S. curruca*) repeatedly sings a harsh jumble of notes followed by a prolonged, monotonous rattle. Blackcaps and garden warblers are among those in which the songs are varied and melodious, often with obvious differences between individuals.

Blackcap songs usually begin slowly, with a jumble of harsh sounding notes, and end with a characteristic series of loud, pure notes. Garden warbler songs are more sustained, with a buzzy quality and lacking a terminal flourish of pure tones. These features can be seen well on sound spectrograms. These are electronically produced traces of the range of frequencies in songs plotted against the song duration. They give a visual impression of the spacing and content of bird songs and other sounds. The songs selected in figure 14 have the above features and show how individual notes are spaced further apart in blackcap than in garden warbler song. Because of this blackcaps sound more relaxed than garden warblers, whose song tempo is distinctly faster.

An important added difference between the two is that the song output of garden warblers is typically much higher. The lengths of the songs are very variable but in Britain, on average, they are similar. For example, 233 blackcap songs timed in Wytham woods, Oxfordshire, averaged 4.07 seconds in duration and 1741 garden warblers songs from the same site averaged 4.06 seconds. However, blackcaps paused for an average of 6.41 seconds between songs and garden warblers had a much shorter song interval of 3.36 seconds. This difference is notice-

caps, which have more time to repeat the breeding cycle since they start sooner in the season and depart later for winter quarters.

PARENTAL CARE

Both sexes in both species share the tasks of incubation and feeding the young. The incubation period is about eleven days for both species. Young garden warblers develop more rapidly than young blackcaps and fledge a day sooner on average, at ten days after hatching. The young of both leave the nest without being able to fly and often assemble inside the shelter of a large shrub where they are fed by the parents for fourteen days or more after leaving the nest.

11

10. *A blackcap nest in brambles.*

11. *A garden warbler nest in brambles.*

12. *A garden warbler brings a caterpillar to its tiny young.*

13. *A half-feathered garden warbler brood is attended by its parents. In both species the adults share parental care.*

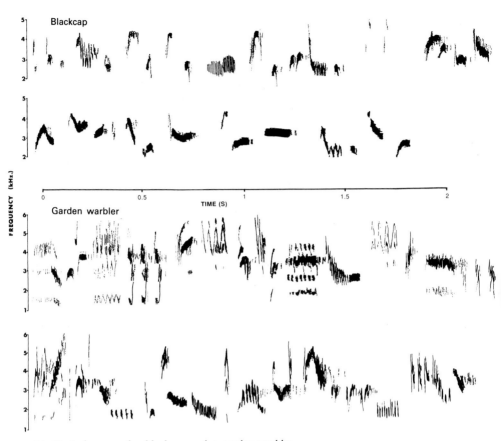

14. *Typical songs of a blackcap and a garden warbler.*

able wherever the two occur and is one of the most reliable ways of telling the species apart.

Distinguishing between the songs is made harder because of their variability. A blackcap courting a female sings an excited continuous chattering song at a fast rate and without the measured ending of pure notes. Such a blackcap can often sound remarkably like a garden warbler. The problem is made worse because blackcaps are accomplished mimics and they may include a garden warbler song in their repertoires if they get the chance to learn it. Similarly, although garden warblers do not have the same reputation as mimics, they sometimes do sound very like typical black-

caps. Figure 15 shows the song of an Oxfordshire garden warbler which sometimes ended its songs with a pure note sequence almost identical to that of a nearby blackcap although, as the spectrogram clearly shows, the typical faster tempo of the garden warbler song remained. In general it is true to say that, although the two species can sound almost identical, a bird will always reveal its true identity provided one listens to the song for long enough.

Various reasons have been put forward to explain why the two birds sound so similar. Many male birds sing not only to advertise the whereabouts of their territories to potential rivals but also to attract mates. For this reason, the songs of different species are generally distinctive, to assist females to find 'their' males. Even highly similar and closely related birds, such as chiffchaffs (*Phylloscopus collybita*) and willow warblers (*P. trochilus*), usually have unmistakably distinct songs. It has been suggested that the normal rule does not apply to blackcaps and garden warblers because song similarity between the two species actually helps to encourage aggression between them. This keeps the birds, which are potential competitors for food and nest sites, apart from each other. Whether or not this is so is hard to establish but an alternative idea seems at least as likely. This is that the songs are similar because their characteristics are related to the nature of the habitat which the birds occupy. For advertising purposes, a song must travel some distance and there is experimental evidence that the songs of these two species are particularly suitable for penetrating the dense undergrowth and scrub which they both favour. In other words, the two sound similar because both songs are an adaptation to the same habitat.

A variation of typical blackcap song is reported from mainland Europe. This is the *Leiern*, in which songs end with a monotonous fluting note, repeated several times. This is monosyllabic or sometimes disyllabic, recalling the 'teacher' song of the great tit (*Parus major*). The *Leiern* is a constant feature of the song of the Iberian blackcaps, is well known in France and Germany, and is sometimes reported further north.

It is often said that blackcaps sing from high, exposed perches and that garden warblers do so from low down in dense cover. This is only true to the extent that a higher proportion of garden warbler territories are in scrub, where only relatively low cover exists. Woodland garden warblers can often be seen singing from perches high in the canopy. *Sylvia* warblers such as the Dartford warbler (*S. undata*) and the Sardinian warbler (*S. melanocephala*), which inhabit very low vegetation, use striking vertical song flights to advertise their territories, but these are not seen in species inhabiting taller cover, including blackcaps and garden warblers. Neither species habitually sings in flight, although both will do so on occasion, especially when flying towards a potential intruder into their territories.

The song period of both species is centred upon the breeding season. Males sing persistently immediately on arrival in the breeding habitat, as they set up territories and try to attract mates. Song output declines after pairing but generally both species sing in the early mornings throughout the breeding season. An evening peak in song output is also

15. *A song ending sung by a blackcap compared with the same notes sung by a nearby garden warbler, which was probably mimicking it.*

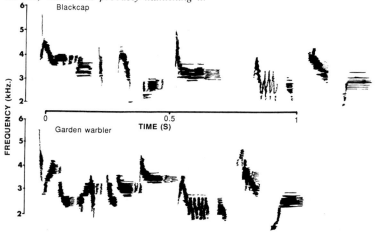

15

16. *A male blackcap inspects its well-feathered young. This brood is close to fledging and would abandon the nest if disturbed. The brown caps of the young are obvious.*

noticeable but is less marked. In Britain, the song period of blackcaps is longer than that of garden warblers. Here blackcaps sing throughout April, May and June, and into July. Garden warbler song output is highest in May, immediately after arrival, declines during June and is inconspicuous later. The difference probably relates to the scarcity of double broods in British garden warblers. Unlike them, a small proportion of British blackcaps have second broods and these birds proclaim and defend their territories by song throughout July and sometimes into August. Blackcaps often sing in winter quarters in Spain and elsewhere, but the importance of this has not been studied, although it is likely to be associated with the maintenance of feeding territories. Similar observations have been made for both species in tropical Africa.

CALLS

Although only the males sing, both sexes of both species have a range of other vocalisations. In particular the 'tac-tac' calls of blackcaps are very distinctive and are given at a high rate when the birds are alarmed or excited. The calls also seem to serve as a 'keep-out' signal when a blackcap is defending a source of food. Blackcaps taking nectar from aloes or goat willows, and sometimes those feeding on fruiting bushes or at bird-tables, may defend the food supply against all comers, including apparently robust rivals such as great tits and robins. The defending blackcap always 'tacs' noisily if other birds appear and chases them away if they continue to approach. The garden warbler equivalent to the 'tac' of blackcaps is a nasal-sounding 'check-check', which is heard particularly when a predator is approaching a nest. Both species have a churring note and blackcaps also often make mewing sounds, sometimes combined with the 'tac' call. In Spain these 'mew-tacs' of blackcaps are often heard in winter when a number are feeding in fruiting olives and other shrubs, but their functional significance is unknown.

Territorial behaviour

Blackcaps and garden warblers are strongly territorial in the breeding season. In both species the breeding territory includes the nest site and up to about one hectare of the surrounding habitat. Territory sizes are smaller where the birds are closely packed in dense scrub and largest in open woodland where the undergrowth is less extensive. It appears that the territory provides a large proportion of the food of a pair and its offspring, as well as the nest site itself.

Territories are established by the males soon after they return from winter quarters. The first male blackcaps to arrive in northern woodlands wander over large areas, singing as they go, but gradually concentrating their movements on the area where they will finally settle. Later arrivals do not do this, at least not overtly, since the choice of possible territories is reduced by the presence of previously established birds. Most garden warblers arrive much later than many blackcaps, although the arrival periods overlap. Typical dates for central England would be 15th April for the first major arrival of blackcaps and 1st May for the garden warblers. The garden warblers rapidly find territories and settle to breed, their relatively late arrival probably accounting for the absence of the leisurely process of territory establishment seen in early blackcaps. In fact, whereas the first male blackcaps are often several days in advance of the first females, male and female garden warblers may be paired from the first day of arrival.

Many migrants show philopatry, that is fidelity to previous breeding or wintering sites. The extent to which blackcaps and garden warblers do this during the breeding season has been studied in several countries. About 30 per cent of garden warblers in an English study site returned to the same general area the next year. A Finnish study of garden warblers showed the same return rate. Blackcaps in Germany showed a return rate of 40 per cent but by contrast less than 5 per cent of the blackcaps at an English site were ever seen again once they had migrated. Such birds as do return often occupy almost the identical spot in successive years. One male garden warbler ringed near Oxford in 1978 occupied the same territory in both 1979 and 1980. Moreover, he was paired to the same female for the first two years, probably an infrequent event in a small passerine given the high mortality rate on migration.

Fidelity to winter quarters has attracted less attention but over several years an average of 9 per cent of blackcaps wintering in Gibraltar returned there for a subsequent winter. Equally, some birds were proved, by ringing there, to winter in later years in completely different areas further north or south. It seems likely that both species are faithful to areas in which they have bred or wintered successfully and in which there is, therefore, a good chance of further success, but that they are versatile enough to move elsewhere if necessary.

INTERSPECIFIC TERRITORIALITY

Blackcaps and garden warblers not only defend their territories against members of their own species: both of them are strongly interspecifically territorial. Blackcaps will not allow garden warbler territories to overlap significantly with their own and in the same way garden warblers exclude blackcaps. The effect is clearly seen if the territories of the two species are plotted in an area where both are breeding. The territories form a mosaic, with little or no overlap between the two species (figure 17). However, if the territories of both are replotted for the same area in other years, the lack of overlap still occurs but often the two species may be occupying different sites

17. *Blackcap and garden warbler territories in an area of mixed deciduous woodland in Oxfordshire in May. The territories of the two species show little overlap.*

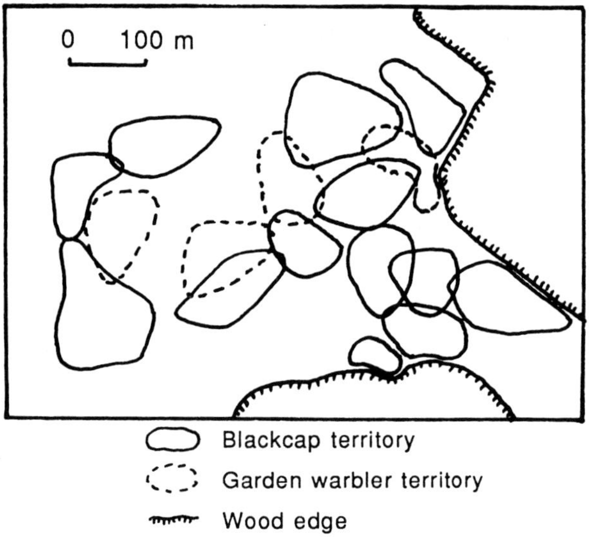

0 100 m
Blackcap territory
Garden warbler territory
Wood edge

18. *Garden warbler territories in an Oxfordshire wood after blackcaps were removed. The area held twice as many garden warblers as when blackcaps were also present (see figure 17).*

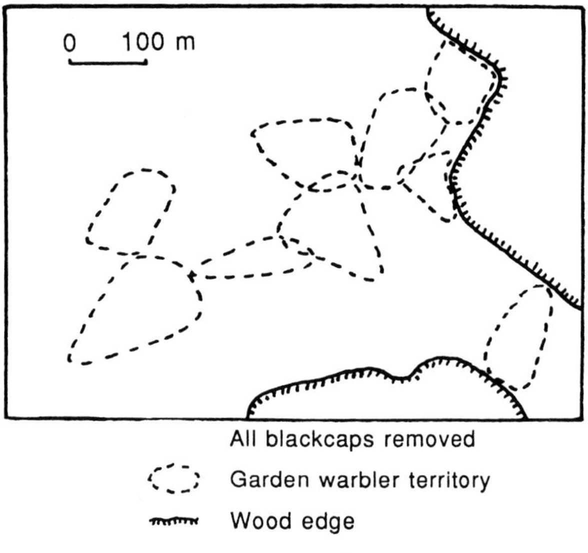

0 100 m
All blackcaps removed
Garden warbler territory
Wood edge

within the area. This emphasises that the territories do not overlap because the birds avoid each other and not because the two species choose different habitats.

TERRITORY DEFENCE

In the first instance territories are defended by song. The voice of the owner is a signal that an area is occupied and it deters intrusion by birds still looking for a place to settle. Like most birds, males immediately approach a loudspeaker playing a recording of the song of their own species. They may sing at the loudspeaker and usually they search the area around it intently, searching for the

19. *A male blackcap displays aggressively during a territorial dispute, making itself conspicuous with raised wings and spread tail as well as by song.*

apparent intruder. The mutual antipathy between blackcaps and garden warblers is confirmed by the finding that they also respond aggressively to recordings of each other's songs. Interestingly, experiments in Britain have shown that blackcaps respond to garden warbler song, as well as to blackcap song, throughout April and May and into June. Blackcaps which are still on territory later in the season continue to respond to blackcap songs but not to those of garden warblers. Perhaps this is because typically garden warblers have finished breeding by early July and afterwards no longer pose a threat to blackcap territories. Garden warbler responses to blackcap song disappear after June, when the garden warbler broods have fledged.

If a rival male approaches a territory boundary there will often be prolonged singing bouts across the border. Occa-

sionally, a male trying to establish itself will trespass on the territories of another. If this happens it will be attacked by the owner, which flies straight at the intruder and usually succeeds in driving it away, although prolonged chasing and vigorous mutual singing may first take place. Actual physical contact during these fights is uncommon but it does occur if an intruder stands its ground. It is uncommon for an occupier of either species to be driven off its territory by a newcomer and this probably explains why most fights are brief affairs, the invader soon realising that it would be better to look for vacant habitat elsewhere.

It might be expected that garden warblers would have to be particularly aggressive in order to claim some living space, given that they have to compete with pre-established blackcaps. A similar situation exists between reed warblers (*Acrocephalus scirpaceus*) and sedge warblers (*A. schoenobaenus*), where the later-arriving reed warblers do sometimes displace sedge warblers from their territories and so secure them for themselves. Reed warblers have a size advantage over sedge warblers. On the other hand, although blackcaps and garden warblers are apparently evenly matched, they do differ conspicuously in aggressiveness, with blackcaps most commonly being dominant. Both defend their territories vigorously and effectively against conspecifics. However, in an English study area, unestablished blackcap males were seen to intrude on garden warbler territories more than twice as often as garden warblers intruded on blackcaps. Some of these intruding blackcaps would seek out and chase the resident garden warblers. On the other hand, garden warblers which ventured into blackcap territories never approached the owners but instead withdrew almost at once when approached by the blackcaps. It is clear that British blackcaps are much more aggressive than garden warblers but still they rarely succeed in displacing established garden warblers although they effectively prevent new garden warbler arrivals from invading their territories. Interestingly, there is evidence that in Finland, where garden warblers are much the more numerous of the two, blackcaps are still the more aggressive species. On the other hand, it has been claimed that in Sweden the opposite is the case: Swedish garden warblers are dominant to the local blackcaps. If this really is the case it warrants closer study since it may help to show in what circumstances it pays either species to be aggressive or relatively retiring.

COMPETITION FOR SPACE

Since blackcaps normally arrive well in advance of garden warblers, the existence of interspecific territoriality implies that the presence of the blackcaps limits the choice of habitat available to garden warblers. Experiments were carried out in an Oxfordshire wood to establish this. An area of open woodland was selected, where five garden warblers and nine blackcaps had held territories the previous year. In the experimental year, all the blackcaps which were present when the first garden warblers arrived were removed. The birds were caught by mist-netting, ringed and released unharmed in another wood. None of them returned to where they were caught. By the end of the season 23 blackcaps had been removed, most of them birds which had tried to fill the vacancies which had been created. However, nine garden warblers established themselves and more than half of their territories were in areas previously occupied by blackcaps (figure 18). Removing blackcaps thus creates vacancies which extra garden warblers will fill if they can, and the distribution of garden warblers is partly determined by that of the more aggressive blackcaps. The conclusion of the experiment was supported by observations the following year, when no birds were artificially removed and when the site was occupied by eleven blackcaps and just four garden warblers.

Both blackcap and garden warbler territories commonly overlap with those of a wide range of other bird species. In northern woodlands these will include such birds as tits, thrushes and *Phylloscopus* warblers. Blackcaps and garden warblers tolerate all these species but not each other. Blackcaps are also intolerant of whitethroats and Sardinian warblers, in England and southern Spain respec-

tively. It is believed that interspecific territoriality is a response to the presence of a strong competitor. As has been described, blackcaps and garden warblers are very similar ecologically, eating much the same food and requiring almost identical nest sites. For this reason, they are unable to tolerate the close proximity of each other.

It may be asked why blackcaps and garden warblers have not evolved greater differences which would allow them to coexist peacefully. Perhaps originally the two were better separated by habitat. The blackcap was a species living in tall forests and the garden warbler a forest-edge species or an inhabitant of open woodlands. Now, as a result of human activities, woodland habitats are mainly small patches with denser and more open stands mixed up with each other, so bringing the two species together. On the other hand, it may be that both retain fairly broad habitat preferences so as to be able to cope with the diversity of vegetation which they must meet on migration and in winter quarters as well as during the breeding season. Lack of specialisation in habitat requirements also allows both blackcaps and garden warblers to take advantage of vacant habitat arising when a rival species suffers particularly high mortality on migration, since this varies greatly from year to year.

Migration

All garden warbler, and most blackcap, populations are strongly migratory, abandoning their breeding ranges during the northern winter. Mediterranean blackcaps, and those living on the Atlantic islands such as Madeira, are sedentary. British blackcaps are migratory and the increasing numbers of blackcaps which winter in Britain are not local birds but instead come from central European populations.

In Europe, the migratory populations of both species show a migratory divide. Ringing recoveries show that the western populations of blackcaps generally fly southwest in autumn to Iberia, whereas those from beyond about 10 to 11 degrees east fly south-east through the eastern Mediterranean region. The migratory divide of garden warblers is situated in the same part of central Europe. However, garden warblers from Scandinavia and Finland also tend to move south-west in autumn into Iberia, whereas blackcaps from the same area tend to take the south-easterly route. Having reached the Mediterranean both species then reorientate southwards to enter Africa.

Planetarium experiments with garden warblers have provided particular information on migratory behaviour. Here birds are shown patterns of the night sky, which they use to orientate, and records are kept of the direction of their movements in the cages. German garden warblers tested in August and September, when they are normally about to leave the breeding quarters, show a strong preference to fly south-west. By October, however, the same birds spend their time trying to fly south, that is, gathering at the south side of the cages. This shows that they have a built-in sense of direction which initially serves to get them south-west to Iberia and then allows them to reorientate south to continue to winter quarters in tropical Africa. Such an innate sense of timing and direction is crucial. If birds did not reorientate successfully in Iberia they would continue south-west and perish in the Atlantic. No doubt some do.

The return movement is less clearly known. Since few are ringed in Africa, natural mortality means that there are fewer ringed birds on the northward passage to provide the information. However, there is some evidence that birds fly on a broad front, across the Sahara and the Mediterranean.

The migration periods of both species differ. Some blackcaps, especially juveniles, begin to leave northern and central Europe in August but most do not do so until September and October, and substantial blackcap passage is recorded by British bird observatories during November. Large numbers of blackcaps are recorded in Gibraltar and Malta from October onwards, although the largest numbers do not appear in Malta until mid December. Apparently the passage south of those birds which winter in the Mediterranean region is a relatively leisurely process, perhaps in response to the gradual depletion of fruit and other food further north.

In contrast, southward migration of garden warblers is relatively early, most leaving the breeding grounds in August and September. British garden warblers leave early, mainly in August, but Scandinavian garden warblers pass through eastern Britain in large numbers in September and into October. Nearly all have crossed the Mediterranean by late October and only a few are recorded there into early November. Garden warblers become common in southern Africa from October onwards, although there are exceptional August records from Malawi and Zambia. Some of these garden warblers have lingered in the northern tropics before continuing their journey south. In Central Nigeria garden warblers begin to arrive from mid September onwards, most of them appearing in October and early November. By late November, however, all have departed further south.

The return passage of both species is more rapid. Blackcaps leave winter quarters earlier. Those wintering in Gibraltar begin to leave early in February. The males depart sooner and, in Gibraltar, are correspondingly laying down fat earlier than the females. Passage through the Mediterranean countries is heavy throughout February and March, with lesser numbers passing in April and stragglers continuing into May. Blackcap passage at south-coast British bird observatories begins in March and is heavy during late April and throughout May. Garden warblers return through the Mediterranean countries during April, May and early June. Some arrive in Britain and north-west Europe from mid April onwards but most passage is in May and some are still moving north in mid June. In both species, the northernmost populations are the latest to arrive in spring and the first to depart in autumn. For example, the bird observatory on Fair Isle, Shetland, handles numbers of Scandinavia-bound warblers in spring and there the peak passage of both species is not until late May and early

June.

It has generally been thought that these species, and other migrant passerines, carry out their migrations by taking on substantial fat reserves and then moving in large stages, perhaps even crossing the Sahara desert and the Mediterranean sea in one continuous flight, a journey of some 2500 km (1500 miles). Recent studies of garden warblers specifically suggest that this may not be so and that, instead, the journeys may be less spectacular, involving shorter flights with frequent stops. Observations in the Sahara suggest that the oases there play an important part in allowing birds to replenish their reserves en route. Garden warblers caught in the Sahara have been tested for their patterns of activity. Heavy birds with good fat deposits tend to be inactive during the day but lean individuals, which need to deposit more fat, spend their time looking for food. During the night the fat birds become restless, suggesting that this is the time when they would normally migrate, but lean birds are inactive, roosting until daylight renews feeding opportunities. It seems, therefore, that garden warblers, and probably other passerine migrants also, cross the Sahara by flying at night,

20. *A female blackcap dangles from a limestick, set by Cypriot bird catchers. Twigs covered in sticky bird lime are put in bushes and birds which perch on them are held fast.*

when it is cooler and they lose less body water. They land during the day, to rest in the shade if their body fuel store in the form of fat reserves is still adequate or to look for food and lay on extra fat if they need it. Birds cross the Mediterranean only when they have adequate reserves for the whole crossing. The fatty fruits found in Mediterranean countries are important to both species as they prepare for the crossing.

Migration is a risky business and mortality is certainly high. The fact that any species migrates at all, however, is evidence that natural selection favours this behaviour. In other words, staying behind would mean even greater mortality so the journeys are worth the high risks. It is a pity that human activities magnify the dangers. Both species are favoured quarry of bird catchers in the Mediterranean region, especially in Italy, Malta, Cyprus and Greece, which are reliably estimated to account for some 900 million migrant birds every year. Millions of blackcaps and garden warblers are included in this unnecessary slaughter. Many of the tiny corpses are pickled in jars and are regarded as a local delicacy. There is no way of knowing whether this persecution has a significant effect on the populations involved but it may not be unimportant. It is to be hoped that an increasing awareness of the need for conservation will lead to an end of the persecution.

Populations

Blackcaps and garden warblers are successful species since they are widespread and numerous. Neither has been censused across its entire range, but the numbers are certainly high. For example, garden warblers are among the commonest birds of the Scandinavian birch forests in summer. The breeding bird atlas for Britain and Ireland suggests that those countries supported some 200,000 pairs of blackcaps and 100,000 pairs of garden warblers in the late 1970s, the great majority of both being in mainland Britain.

22

The best estimates for the global populations of both species are based on average densities of breeding birds compared with the known total extent of the habitats which they use. It has been suggested that the post-breeding population of garden warblers is of the order of 380 million birds and that of blackcaps 340 million birds. However, it has to be stressed that these figures are largely speculative and in any event the populations of both fluctuate considerably from year to year.

National censuses also provide information on changes in numbers of bird species and here there are interesting patterns of difference. The Common Birds Census of the BTO monitors changes in the numbers of these and other species annually. The results show that in Britain there has been a substantial and continuing increase in blackcaps. Garden warblers correspondingly declined during the 1960s and 1970s but recovered strongly during the 1980s, when woodland populations have been high. In blackcaps, especially, changes have been most marked on farmland, where the habitat is less suitable.

In both species the preferred woodland habitat is presumably filled first, with numbers being high on farmland only when the woodland populations are also high. There are anecdotal reports from various parts of Britain that when blackcaps are common in a particular wood garden warblers are relatively scarce there, but that the positions may be reversed in other years. This would be an expected result of interspecific territoriality and a long-term study is needed to confirm it. Otherwise there is as yet no evidence that the numbers of one species are in any way regulated by the numbers of the other, although if blackcaps continue to increase it is to be expected that garden warblers may find themselves restricted in choice of habitat.

Within Britain, blackcaps have become progressively commoner in the north. At the beginning of the twentieth century garden warblers were the commoner species in counties such as Yorkshire and Lancashire. Now blackcaps outnumber them there and in virtually all the other English counties. Similar increases in blackcaps have been documented for Finland, Norway and Sweden and there have been big increases in the numbers of blackcaps recorded on migration at some bird observatories, particularly in Britain and Holland. There is good evidence, therefore, that blackcap populations in northern Europe enjoyed healthy growth during the 1970s and 1980s. Garden warbler populations seem to have remained comparatively stable generally but with signs of an increase in the late 1980s especially.

The different winter quarters of the two species may affect their survival in different ways. The droughts in the Sahel zone of North Africa, which decimated their close relative the whitethroat in the late 1970s, may have caused high mortality in both species but especially in garden warblers, as all the latter have to cross this zone on migration. However, since neither species winters there, they have escaped the fate of the whitethroats, the populations of which have been drastically reduced. The tendency of many blackcaps to winter north of the Sahara may have helped their survival and may account for some of the increases seen in north-west Europe. This period of increase has been accompanied by an added tendency for some to winter as far north as Britain, perhaps encouraged by a succession of mild winters in the 1970s and 1980s. Until 1958 all blackcaps ringed in south-west Germany were recovered from more southerly locations. Recoveries from areas to the north and north-west, in the Netherlands, Belgium and the British Isles, began to become more frequent during the period 1959 to 1970 and made up 27 per cent of all recoveries during 1976 to 1980. In Britain, wintering blackcap records averaged 22 a year during 1945 to 1954, increasing to 380 a year by 1970 to 1977 and to 1714 in 1978 to 1979. As the trend progressed the birds became more widespread. At first, wintering blackcaps were largely confined to southern and south-western England. By the 1980s they were commonly being recorded throughout the country, even wintering in Orkney and Shetland in the far north.

Whether this behaviour will continue if colder winters return is of course unknown but since blackcaps have become used to garden bird-tables they may be able to cope with hard weather.

Further reading

Bairlein, F. 'The Migratory Strategy of the Garden Warbler: A Summary of Field and Laboratory Data', *Ringing and Migration*, 8 (1987), 59-72.

Garcia, E. F. J. 'An Experimental Test of Competition for Space between Blackcaps and Garden Warblers in the Breeding Season', *Journal of Animal Ecology*, 52 (1983), 795-805.

Garcia, E. F. J. 'Warbler (1)', in B. Campbell and E. Lack (editors), *A Dictionary of Birds*, T. and A. D. Poyser, 1985.

Howard, H. E. *The British Warblers*. R. H. Porter, 1907-14.

Lack, P. *The Atlas of Wintering Birds in Britain and Ireland*. T. and A. D. Poyser, 1986.

Langslow, D. R. 'Recent Increases of Blackcaps at Bird Observatories', *British Birds*, 71 (1978), 345-54.

Langslow, D. R. 'Movements of Blackcaps Ringed in Britain and Ireland', *Bird Study*, 26 (1979), 239-52.

Leach, I. 'Wintering Blackcaps in Britain and Ireland', *Bird Study*, 28 (1981), 5-14.

Mason, C. F. 'Breeding Biology of the Sylvia Warblers', *Bird Study*, 23 (1976), 213-32.

Moreau, R. E. *The Palearctic-African Bird Migration Systems*. Academic Press, London and New York, 1972.

Sharrock, J. T. R. (editor). *The Atlas of Breeding Birds in Britain and Ireland*. British Trust for Ornithology, Tring, Hertfordshire, 1976.

Simms, E. *British Warblers*. Collins, 1985.

Williamson, K. *Identification for ringers: 3. The Genus Sylvia*. BTO Field Guide number 9, 1976.

ACKNOWLEDGEMENTS

I am most grateful to Dr Euan Dunn for his valued comments on the manuscript. Data from the Nest Record scheme and the Common Birds Census of the British Trust for Ornithology are used by kind permission of the Director, Dr Jeremy Greenwood. Photographs are acknowledged as follows: Eric and David Hosking, 3, 4, 9, 12, 13, 16, 19, cover (John Hawkins); ICBP, 20 (Gernant Magnin); Frank Lane Picture Agency, 1 (Hans Dieter Brandl); M. C. Wilkes, 6; Graham J. Wren, 10, 11.